YOUR KNOWLEDGE HAS VALUE

- We will publish your bachelor's and master's thesis, essays and papers

- Your own eBook and book - sold worldwide in all relevant shops

- Earn money with each sale

Upload your text at www.GRIN.com and publish for free

Sanam Mukhtar

About the Impact of Technology upon Society

GRIN Verlag

Bibliografische Information der Deutschen Nationalbibliothek:

Die Deutsche Bibliothek verzeichnet diese Publikation in der Deutschen Nationalbibliografie; detaillierte bibliografische Daten sind im Internet über http://dnb.d-nb.de/ abrufbar.

Dieses Werk sowie alle darin enthaltenen einzelnen Beiträge und Abbildungen sind urheberrechtlich geschützt. Jede Verwertung, die nicht ausdrücklich vom Urheberrechtsschutz zugelassen ist, bedarf der vorherigen Zustimmung des Verlages. Das gilt insbesondere für Vervielfältigungen, Bearbeitungen, Übersetzungen, Mikroverfilmungen, Auswertungen durch Datenbanken und für die Einspeicherung und Verarbeitung in elektronische Systeme. Alle Rechte, auch die des auszugsweisen Nachdrucks, der fotomechanischen Wiedergabe (einschließlich Mikrokopie) sowie der Auswertung durch Datenbanken oder ähnliche Einrichtungen, vorbehalten.

Imprint:

Copyright © 2013 GRIN Verlag GmbH
Druck und Bindung: Books on Demand GmbH, Norderstedt Germany
ISBN: 978-3-656-35198-6

This book at GRIN:

http://www.grin.com/en/e-book/205584/about-the-impact-of-technology-upon-society

GRIN - Your knowledge has value

Der GRIN Verlag publiziert seit 1998 wissenschaftliche Arbeiten von Studenten, Hochschullehrern und anderen Akademikern als eBook und gedrucktes Buch. Die Verlagswebsite www.grin.com ist die ideale Plattform zur Veröffentlichung von Hausarbeiten, Abschlussarbeiten, wissenschaftlichen Aufsätzen, Dissertationen und Fachbüchern.

Visit us on the internet:

http://www.grin.com/

http://www.facebook.com/grincom

http://www.twitter.com/grin_com

Abstract

Technology has improved the general living standards of many people in the last few decades. Without technology, people would still be living within their geographical confines of their societies. Examples of technological advancements that have made life easier include things like the Internet, phones, tablets, TV, PS and movie and video games. However, these are just the positive attributes of technology; there are also a number of negative effects that it has brought upon the society in general. This research paper seeks to discuss these negative impacts of technology upon the society and the general way of living. Arguably, some of these technological advancements have increased stress levels and isolation within the society. As it appears, technology has had a rational impact on the meaning of "social". It has touched many different aspects of life including education, communication, transport, war, and even fashion. Many in the society are worried about the rapid transformation in human attention.

Introduction

The term technology lightens up the faces of many people especially the young generation. Life has improved in the last few decades since technology has evolved at an incredibly fast rate. It is now hard to imagine life without technology, which includes things like the Internet, phones, tablets, TV, PS and movie and video games. While people embrace this positive attributes of technology, they tend to forget many negative effects it has brought upon the society in general. One would quickly think thank such technological tools have improved human lives because they have enabled people to gain an understanding of other civilizations, meet with different people on a global scale, preserve or reinforce familial relationships, be in touch with the rest of the society, and help individuals to become socially adroit. Nevertheless, some of these technological aspects increase stress levels and isolation in the society. As it appears, technology has had a rational impact on the meaning of "social".

Technological experts are worried about the rapid transformation in human attention. They have also raised alarm concerning people's future ability to deal with intricate challenges. In view, the impact of a different future because of multitasking and short-term mindset will be negative because the social encouragement for profound engagement will eventually come to a halt. Undeniably, technology has also changed the way teachers teach in classrooms. Ever since its introduction, various efforts have been channeled towards helping educators and the different means of implementing such in the classroom situation. They had

voiced concern with the introduction of the use of technologies in the classroom such as laptops, handheld technologies, computers, digital movies, and video content.
Students nowadays face constant exposure to different forms of media, which then impacts on the way they use information and interact with each other. These new technological advancements have drastically changed the teacher student dynamics. The central role that has always been played by the classroom instructor is fading away. Now the instructor acts as a middleman linking information to students. Students are now actively involved with the procurement, designing, rearranging, and displaying of vital information. By any mean, the introduction of technologies has minimized the rank of teachers in the classroom situation. This essay looks at various negative effects of technology on all aspects of human life.

Negative Effects of Technology

Undeniably, the numerous advancements in technology being churned out every day have been helpful. The last few decades have seen technology evolve at an incredibly fast rate unimagined before. Cell phones are now performing tasks that were originally assigned to a computer. It is now hard to imagine life without things like the Internet, email, Facebook, or other chat features on phones and tablets. Other technological gadgets like TV, PS and movie or video games have also evolved over time, each offer its consumers a variety of choices and novel possibilities. However, despite the publicity and positive advancements and achievements brought about by modern technology, many do not realize the impact and negative effects it has brought to people and society in general. Arguably, a number of technological advancements have adversely affected definite industrial sectors, like the print media. These advancements have even caused several businesses to shut down forever or shift their scope of business because there is a lack of demand for their type of goods and services.

Newspaper businesses and local agencies have been hit hard; some have been forced to shut down or lay off a large chunk of their employees because news these days is readily available on the Internet, especially on the social media. Several companies and other businesses now depend deeply on digital printing means for magazines, brochures, as well as, other advertisement supplies they require, thereby putting conventional, lithographic printing in a tough spot. Music lovers do not have to purchase their favorite singles or albums from music stores anymore, many files are readily accessible over the Internet, a phenomenon that has forced big music store companies to shut down or shift their mode of businesses.

Consequently, the movie industry has also suffered since consumers can now download or purchase movies online, which has decreased DVD sales.

There is no denying that technology has its positive attributes, but when looking at the way it has impacted on the society, especially the way people interact with each other, then it is safe to state that technology has a negative impact. Modern technology has changed the way people interact nowadays. One can communicate with whomever at any given time using the many social media platforms present to date. This sounds like a helpful idea, but it has created a distinct barrier because people have ceased to interact the on a personal basis like the traditional way. As a result, people are becoming confined to their homes, and do not want to interact with the outside world. Many fun games like football, basketball or tennis can now be played online; therefore, people have ceased to anticipate going outside and playing such games with their friends. While technology is vital in making life easier, interaction with the rest of the society is important; becoming desensitized to the public is harmful.

Without looking at the bigger picture, one would quickly think that these technological tools have enabled people to gain an understanding of other civilizations, meet with different people on a global scale, preserve or reinforce familial relationships, be in touch with the rest of the society, and help individuals to become socially adroit. Nonetheless, some technological aspects increase stress levels and isolation in the society. It is common nowadays to be involved in relationships via technology, but at times, the quantity of such associations leaves individuals involved feeling somehow empty. Technology has had a philosophical impact on the meaning of the term "social". If it has not already happened; therefore, it is crucial to redefine socially tolerable and suitable behaviors in view of virtual and digital interaction. At this point in time, very few have critically thought about the novel social realities that have come with technology, as well as, the meaning of these realities in view of the person as well as the society.

A recent study about information technology and students pointed out that a majority of undergraduates used social networking sites, including Twitter, Face book, MySpace, and Instagram, among many more others. About 85 percent of the respondents stated that they used such social platforms on a daily basis. This report points out one defining factor: that the use of these sites is on an upward trend. Notably, using these sites has both positive and negative impacts. It enables long lost pals or family members to reconnect and keep in touch. This is convenient considering relationships that are usually geographically alienated However, one should not look beyond their noses to pinpoint the issues that relate to social networking sites. Currently, people are debating on whether it is real that people are addicted to the Internet.

These problems appear to be real. Some argue that such social platforms have added to cheating, which have ended in couples divorcing. Several people have been fired from work or their positions because of statements posted on these sites, which may not have been real or intended. Apart from these, it is uncommon to see egotism manifest on these sites. This refers to the excessive interest in oneself and one's manifestation. Undeniably, some of these sites have become avenues for a certain group of people to show-off their narcissistic characteristics online. One is left wondering whether such people use these platforms to show their popularity to the globe rather than use them to build up momentous relationships. The simple act of sharing common interests and hobbies with other people via technology does not necessarily bring positive effects on social development and social capabilities.

Gaming and Social Advancement

Gaming is one example where one may come face to face with potentially damaging social impediments. People like to play online games, but fail in carrying out any deep, reverential and meaningful conversations. Bauchspies, Croissant, & Restivo (2005) point out the negative social impacts of certain video games. An insight by Komblum & Smith (2007) sought to find whether high and long exposure to violent video games increased antagonism over time. They found out that, engaging in violent video games poses a considerable risk factor for afterward aggression in the physical sense for boys and girls in countries like the US and Japan. Nonetheless, this should not mean that people should link poor social skills to video games because other sports and activities might do the same. Nevers (1972) views that, the main problem lies in addiction. Definitely, over indulgence in one activity, in this case, gaming would end deleterious consequences.

Television and Social Advancement

The use of television represents another form of technology with mixed reviews when it comes to social lives and social skills. Baldanf & Stair (2008) view that, limited watching of certain programs may strengthen friendships of family ties. Nonetheless, others like Komblum & Smith (2007) suggest that, the TV set adds to the downfall of societal values in a number of technologically advanced countries. The amount of time people spend watching programmes of TV is not proportional to their family time. For that reason, television offers no meaningful opportunity for positive interaction while viewing. Television watchers just have to sit and consume all the things presented to them without reacting or responding to other persons. In the end, this can seriously affect individual social skills since viewers cannot practice or engage in a meaningful relationship with other people. Arguably, exposure to certain programmes on TV sets can come with adverse effects on the social lives of families (Bergen, Reid, & Torelli, 2007). For instance, exposure to programmes with explicit sexual content can increase cases of teenage pregnancies. Moreover, sexual, violent, and lascivious programming on television may make people become prone to such behavior since they see it as acceptable behavior in the community. If everyone was to mimic such behaviors shown on certain television programmes, then the society would be meaningless since it would lack morals, law and order. Consequently, majority of individual lives would be blemished. Apparently, technology can present either meaningful or harmful effects on the social life and social skills of people.

On another scale, Chapelle (2003) shares her apprehension regarding transformation in human attention, as well as, the depth of discourse among the young generation immersed under the influence of hyperconnectivity. Some like Goyder (2005) have also raised alarm regarding people's future ability to deal with intricate challenges. The short spans of attention from quick interaction characteristic with new technology may be damaging to focusing on the more complex issues, which may lead to stagnation in areas such as literature and overall technology. As the emphasis placed on social exchanges moves from the current to the next, many will fail to recognize the wisdom and retrospective manifestation it conveys. Green (2002) has predicted that these social systems will fundamentally grow to propose even more support to individuals who can engage in deep-thinking. The impact of a different future as a result of short-term mindset and multitasking will be negative because the social encouragement for profound engagement will eventually grind down.

A number of students have also raised alarm regarding their peers' aptitude to move beyond short-term association to information. Several reports depict people having difficulty with sustaining attention, for example, extensively being engrossed in reading a book. Many young and impressionable minds these days depend on technology for most of important things in their lives. Green (2002) has foreseen a decrease in patience and immediacy amongst many individuals. Individuals who are born with quick access to the Internet and media may be less possible to follow longer routes to uncovering information. They will most likely seek quick fixes than engaging in meaningful and deep investigation before arriving to a conclusion. Technology experts attest to fears that technology is currently taking the overall ability, and consciousness to engage in critical thinking or analysis, and hence individual determinism in contemporary society.

What would such mean for social resiliency? People want to maintain the high levels of attention on a solitary thing for just a few hours. Will things like movies and classical concerts be reduced to something like 30 minutes? At the current trend, it appears that communication will end up becoming more direct; things that may be lost include idle conversation and supercilious greetings or niceties. Internet based discussion will lean towards being opinion-based, pithy and shared via social media platform, rather than challenging.

More and more, the young and upcoming generation will rely on the first amount of information they come across about a topic, with the assumption that it is the right answer, rather than using vetting and context to attain a holistic analysis of a subject matter. People are becoming less interested in meaningful human interaction than things they see on social giants like Facebook. Arguably, the relationship between parents and children is deteriorating in favor of pursuit of information online. The next generation will most certainly be different since they will grow up. Such a generation will find it difficult to tackle any complex issues that affect the society in general. Over a long time, the human society has been in dire need of communication.

Innovativeness and creation of value requires a deeper level of interaction than just a bunch of social media postings or tweets. According to Hjorth (2003), deep and meaningful engagement has always let creative individuals solve complex issues. The notion that speediness is a universal remedy for enhanced behavioral, cognitive, and social function is directly conflicting with contemporary movements, which believe that times is an important factor in the capability to create, adapt, collaborate, or gain all the desirable qualities in life.

The argument that technology may be taking humanity down a catastrophic path has some sense. By and large, the current generation has failed to learn to preserve anything than petite bits of information. As CDs, DVDs, IBM, and HP continue to experience dropped sales, cloud computing, nanotechnology, flash drives, and the likes with continue to rule the day. The touchpad over the last few years has blown up exponentially in terms of available application and its usage. In the end, they will become communication media, books and everything else. Face to face contact will be replaced with time spent with touch screen gadgets and cameras. Stagnation of the entire population will become eminent due to lack of deep thinking and innovativeness. The desire to accomplish basic human drives will be lost. Several people have also raised health concerns because people can prefer to be in the chat rooms. Nevers (1972) views that, the obesity in developed nations will be on the increase. There will be a vast availability of fast food and unhealthy eating diets. Many young teenagers are unable to function without direct access to social affirmation and online sources. Expressing information is slowly being replaced with emoticons and flaming. The amount of knowledge about history, politics, science, and culture is being replaced with knowledge on pop culture. It appears that people from the next generation will take it as a challenge to separate the truth from lies. The ability to process information at a deeper level will be lost also.

There are thousands of surveys, researchers and studies that evidently show how children and teenagers are being harmfully impacted when they interact with modern technology. The documented affects of video games, cell phones, iPads, DVDs, and many more others, on children and teenagers is undeniably atrocious. Most of the such negative impacts are as a result of these children withdrawing from any conventional form of social interaction or physical exercises. Only one form of technology, the camera, can force this group of youngsters into venturing on the outside. The good thing with the use of cameras is that it forces the participant to interrelate directly with the outside world.

Cameras and photography in general enhance and sharpen creative thinking, develop observational skills, which eventually lets the young generation reconnect with the outside world and explore the beauty and mysteries of nature. According to technology experts, the digital camera functions differently from other technological inventions like the computer, TV, MP3 player, video game, cell phone, or iPads (Pattavina, 2004). Ever since its invention, the camera encourages every individual who wants to use it to go outside, exercise, and explore the immediate environment. It encourages people to take nature walks in order to bird watch or experience nature first hand. It is the only form of technology that teenagers can use while offering all the positive attributes they overlook while connecting with the rest of the technological forms.

Negative Effects of Technology on the Environment

In the current society, a sizeable number of people work longer hours in search of better pay and advancements in their careers. Clocking longer hours in the office means an increase in the use of new technology, which means more amounts of energy is being exploited. The impact of this chain of events on the ecological system is substantial both positively and negatively. The benefits of modern technology can hardly be denied. There have been several technological advancements, which have come with positive environmental impacts. Even so, it is undeniable that there are numerous negative impacts of the same. Some people have called for the lessening of hours at work, stating that it will have a positive outcome on the environment, as well as the raw materials being depleted every hour. Many people agree with this theory that a reduction in hours will lead to an improved quality of life. However, they still have reservations with the notion that cutting down these hours will minimize the negative impacts on the ecological system.

To counter such an argument, some have argued that reducing these hours will not automatically mean a reduction in the damage brought upon the environment (Bauchspies, Croissant, & Restivo, 2005). Every year, technological innovations have focused on churning out low energy products, which is expected to eventually minimize the damages caused to the environment. Because of such advancements, people argue that there is no dire need to minimize the work hours because the expected reduction in the consumption of energy will even make employees work for more hours. The rate at which the world is consuming and depleting the various sources of energy is alarming. Most businesses use computer technology to run their businesses; therefore, the industrial consumption of energy is continually on the increase. Data from the IEA (International Energy Agency show that approximately 4 percent of the global energy expenditure in the year 2008 was because of the use of ICTs. Furthermore, it is predicted that this figure increases at a fast rate of 40 percent each year by the time it reaches 2030. This means that businesses and corporations will have to look for alternatives to avoid computer technologies from draining the already depleted energy resources. A quick check around the world points out the laxity in major organization in finding more ecologically sound solutions for energy production. To date, most of these companies still have not yet thought of means to improve the carbon footprint they emit to the environment.

Many other environmental and ecological issues that arise are also as a result of newly industrialized nations like China and South Korea. Numerous high technology gadgets found in most modern homes like the microwave and kettles are amongst the largest contributors of harmful products to the environment. The base line is that, industrialization together with recent advancement in technology has greatly continued to negatively impact the environment. The industrial benefits that come from technological adjustment in many activities has ultimately added to the higher living standards; nonetheless, the negative part on technology appear to show more as the years go by. The evidence can be seen all around. There is a considerable increase in international consultations and discussion through meetings and conferences on matters dealing with energy and global warming. Issues and discomfort associated with the negative effects of technology are on the global increase.

In view, one of the things that lead to environmental pollution is the mismanagement of technology and lack of control measures put in place (Baldanf & Stair, 2008). The amplified consumption of these improved things consequently triggers demand, which then manipulates the supply of high quality product that mainly power industrialization with the use of improved technology. The high demand of technology in such cases is an outcome of the need to satisfy human wants and quest. Undesirable environmental pollution, therefore, is eminent because of an increased production in the processing and manufacturing industries; the use of automobiles and dangerous weapons.

Water, air, and noise pollution are the main environmental components that have been affected due to technological advancement. The discharge of huge amounts of dangerous gases like CO_2 into the air by major industries leads to air pollution, which then degrades the environment in a major way. Moreover, the disposal of some of these industrial wastes into water bodies by institutions poses a major environmental disaster via water pollution. Furthermore, environmental dilapidation is also on the increase as a result of similar noise pollution from the use and testing weapons, as well as, the use of locomotives and automobiles on the vast road networks.

According to Ritchel (2010), the use and development of technology is ghastly contributing to the current industrial activities, which need raw material from natural the already depleted natural resources like timber, precious metals, gas, and also wild animals. While the vast agricultural activities in emerging economies like Bangladesh can be beneficial to the whole world, the activities leads to an extensive depletion of natural forest cover, soil fertility, and water. The burning of bushes, clearing of the new forest covers, and use of chemicals to improve soil fertility should be an environmental concern. Also, the extensive mining of precious minerals like diamond, gold, silver, steel and others represent an activity that is very fast adding to the depletion of resources. Notably, these metals are of help, but the overexploitation leads it to become an environmental concern.

Arguably, the disruptions and imbalances seen in the ecological systems come from the recent advancements in technology. In the near future, it will not be shocking to see a total collapse in the ecological life, as well as, the annihilation of organisms. The recent enhanced forms of technology force humanity to look for other convenient means to satisfy their basic human needs. It seems that people have returned to dangerous activities such as extensive farming, deforestation, and environmental pollution, which change the usual lifecycles in the ecosystem. Although ecosystems can come back from such negative effects, it usually takes a very long time; therefore, the nonstop environmental degradation via destructive activities discussed above will eventually end in a total collapse of the ecological system.

In view, ongoing problems related to global warming include a number of environmental factors and negative effects of technological advancements. Hudson (2011) states that, unbridled utilization and advancement of technology in areas that cause water and air pollution lead to imbalances in the atmospheric gases. Emission of dangerous gases to the atmosphere in huge amounts forms greenhouse effects, which mainly contribute to global warming. Greenhouse gases come from human activities such as poor and dangerous farming methods, harmful transport systems, renewable generation of power and manufacturing processes like the use of coal. Extraction of fossil fuel via clearing and burning of farm lands negatively affects climate in an immense way.

Negative Effects of Technology on the Education System

Technology was first introduced into classrooms after the spread of internet in the 1990s. Although technology comes with advancement in knowledge, many educators saw this introduction as a major setback in their line of work. Examples of technologies introduced to the classroom include laptops, handheld technologies, computers, digital movies, and video content. The newest to be introduced and still under creation includes tablets and podcasting. A majority of students, especially in developed and second world countries are facing constant exposure to different forms of media, which then impacts on the way they use information and interact with each other (Kulik, 1994). Notably, both effective teachers and effective use of technology put in to use the evidence base approaches including frequent testing, adaptive content, and sudden feedback. Research carried out in computer related settings pointed out increases in high order and cooperative learning, student center, technological use, problem solving and writing skills.

Furthermore, it also enhances positive attitudes towards the use of technology by teachers, parents and students. Ever since the introduction of new technological advancements, the teacher student dynamics have radically changed based on the structure of the classroom. The central role played by the classroom instructor is fading away (Ausubel & Sladovich, 1999). The instructor is currently acting as a middleman facilitating the passage of information from its source to student. The new student has become active in the procurement, designing, rearranging, and displaying of vital information. According to a study carried out to assess teachers, most of the teachers confessed to being prickly with the use of most of the newly advanced technology. Courts & Tucker (2012) view that, this leaves tech-savvy learners in a position to aid the teachers in the use of technology. Consequently, the introduction of technologies has minimized the rank of teachers in the classroom situation, especially those that belong to a different generation. Students on their end like learning from these technologies and not the conventional chalkboard (Geer & Sweeney, 2012).

Undeniably, there are numerous blessings of IT in the classroom situation; nonetheless, there are also negative effects of the same. Limited access of learning resources to students can be disadvantageous. The educational needs of the entire class may never be realized if there is a limited access to things like video cameras, computers, and whiteboards. The idea of having computer labs in place of classroom computers may pose difficulty to teachers since they will be assigned special computer classes. Technology driven education games and videos are currently being incorporated into the classroom and lives of the young generation. These technological tools are supposed to be used to develop and grow the young minds, as well as, increase their awareness and overall knowledge. According to Sikorsk (2007), there is a conflicting debate on the usefulness of educational videos like Baby Einstein's DVDs.

According to some research, infant vocabulary is slowly reducing as a result of these education baby DVDs (Sivin-Kachala, 1998). The study, done by the Washington University, states that the toddlers who watched the programme ended up knowing about 8 fewer words of the 90 common words pronounced by babies who never watched the DVDs. This may be true because these children are supposed to learn to speak with real people instead of watching DVDs. Such babies will rarely get to experience equal linguistic experience. A group of scholars has also voiced the same sentiments, stating that these baby DVDs are adding no value to the babies, hence may be harmful to them.

Furthermore, a sizeable number of students face the risk of failing in school despite having immense potential to study and excel in life. According to the US Department of Education, their academic qualification in key areas like reading, writing, math, and science fall below their expected potential. There is a lot of evidence showing that such difficulty in studying is cumulative in nature. Basically, the gap between potential and achievement gets bigger from childhood into adolescence. Such young adults have a tendency of dropping out of school more than students without the difficulties stated above. Also, they have to grapple with the effects underemployment and unemployment. Therefore, they face a large risk of experiencing long life issues as a group.

According to Wenglisky (1998), to use technology efficiently in the classroom situation, a lot of training needs to be carried out in ensuring that educators get the best out of it. Technology, if used properly enhances learning; therefore, it only serves rights that educators become comfortable while using it. In the end, students will get the fullest advantages that come with educational technology. Baker, Gearhart, & Herman (1994) agrees to the fact that, current training of technology seems to focus on technological skills and knowledge, but it overlooks the existing relationships between pedagogy, technology and content. In the end, educators learn about the new ideas, but fail to apply it in the classroom situation. It is essential that candidates be availed with ample opportunities to integrate technology into their learning programmes in an efficient way.

Departments of education should, therefore, focus on creating teacher education programmes, which will then bring improvement on students' beliefs, technological skills, and intentions about incorporating technology into class work. Efficient training in technology will openly enhance pre-service teachers' value beliefs and self-efficacy. This in turn, will shape the manner in which students use technology in the classroom situation (Wenglisky, 1998). Consequently, educational planners and educators are left scuffling to catch the ever changing technology. Arguably, a number of technological firms have introduced technology into numerous conventional learning tools to let teachers interact with the fast and swift advances in technology.

Impacts of Technology and New Media on Customer Relationships

Looking around, there is the emergence of new media marketing clearly dominated by new technology like the mobile, recommendation systems, shopping bots, as well as, peer-to-peer networks. According to research it has created a novel online marketplace, which challenges the conventional way of buying and selling. The usual straight line that was a characteristic of customer relationship management appears to have come to a stop. In its place is the zigzag pathway that somehow looks like the famous game of pinball. Notably, this pathway comes with rewards and risks alike, waiting for businesses that want to experience the new online marketplace. Therefore, exploiting such opportunities and evading their respective risks and pitfalls requires the potential customers to get attracted to the new media. Furthermore, it is crucial to comprehend how the market influences consumer behaviors and attitudes. It is crucial to take note of new tactical and strategic marketing techniques, and how they apply to the characteristics shown on the novel media, together the effects they have on the consumers.

According to Harel & Papert (1991), companies that fail to adapt to these new technological advancements will be eventually locked out or be forced to quit altogether. Social networking platforms like YouTube, Facebook, Twitter, and Google avail consumers with a huge role as market players. According to Hudson (2011), customers can be able to be reached by any company at any time at any place. Consumers are armed with Internet tools; therefore, they end up serving as critics on Amazon, writers on Wikipedia, producers on sites like YouTube, and also retailers on market giant eBay. All these aspects pose certain challenges on companies trying to reach or expand their customer base. Customers no longer use their personal computer to make decisions about buying and selling.

New technological advancements like smart phones, iPads, and laptops make real time exchange of information an important part of consumer behavior without the conventional restrictions that were presented some years back. There is no restriction when it comes to geographical boundaries or time of the day. Arguably, this new media is bringing with it enhanced customer relationships. It also increases business via strategies that conform to the new and constantly changing media. However, despite all these, the new media is displacing the conventional corporate strategies and business models that businesses were used to. This shift poses a profound impact on many businesses, which have to constantly study the new market place to ensure they are never left behind.

Conclusion

The text in this paper does not deny that technology has its positive attributes; however, it is the manner at which it has impacted on the society that brings worries. The way people communicate with each other has significantly changed. The invention of the email, Facebook, Twitter, and instant texting means that one can communicate with whomever anytime. This is such a wonderful idea, the problem is it has created a distinct barrier because people no longer interact on a personal basis like it was a few decades back. People are being confined to their homes the more as new technology is being introduced. Perhaps it is worth noting that technology is vital in making life easier, but interaction with the rest of the society is more important. One instance of the negative impacts brought about by technology is gaming. Many kids nowadays know how to fully play even complex game, but fail to participate in any reverential or meaningful conversations. Several studies have sought to find the negative social impacts that come with video games. The problem is definitely full blown because of over indulgence in such gaming activities (Goyder, 2005).

The other instance of misuse of technology is in television. In view, excess watching of television programmes or movies, is evidently and slowly leading to the downfall of societal values. Many people are nowadays spending most of their time watching television than the time they spend bonding with their family or friends. Children in the past used to play outside with the rest of the peers. But it is no more. Furthermore, exposure to certain programmes on TV sets with explicit sexual content can increase cases of teenage pregnancies. Furthermore, sexual, violent, and lascivious programming on television may make individuals become prone to such appalling behavior (Komblum & Smith, 2007).

Media marketing as discussed above has created a new form of the online marketplace. This has proved to challenge the usual way of buying and selling. The conventional straight line has been replaced with a zigzag pathway, which has come with both rewards and risks. The problem comes to those companies that fail to adapt to these new technological advancements. They will be ultimately locked out or be forced to quit from their businesses. New technological advancements have improved real time exchange of information. Arguably, the new media has displaced the usual corporate strategies and business models that businesses were using. Such a profound shift poses unimaginable impact on businesses, which have to constantly study the new market place to ensure they are never left behind.

It is also worth noting the effects of technology in educational systems. There are immense benefits that come with using technology in the educational sector; even so, there is no denying the existence of negative effects of the same. The problem usually comes when there is limited access of learning resources to students. As discussed above, the educational needs of the entire class may never be realized if there is a limited access to things like video cameras, computers, and whiteboards (Bauchspies, Croissant, & Restivo, 2005). A sizeable number of students fail to qualify in important areas like writing, reading, math, and science. Lot of evidence shows a gap between potential and achievement, which gets bigger from childhood into adolescence. These students end up dropping out of school more than their counterparts without such difficulties. Furthermore, they face a high risk of unemployment and underemployment.

Another topic discussed above was the effect of technology on the environment. It is baffling to note the rate at which the sources of energy is consumed. The new inventions in technology are increasingly using huge amounts of energy. Other environmental and ecological issues that arise are also from the current age of the industrial revolution. Despite all these negativity, this text does not advise people or corporations to cease from using technology. As a matter of fact, technology has made life easier than the last many decades. What needs to be done is careful and restricted use of technology. The society should take up the positive attributes of technology and leave out those that affect the conventional way of life. Companies should also look for ways to reduce the rate of environmental damage brought about by the new technological advancements.

References

Ausubel, J., & Sladovich, A. (1999). *Technological Advancement.* Washington DC, US: National Academic Publishers.

Baker, E., Gearhart, M., & Herman, J. (1994). *Technology Assessment in Education and Training* . Hillsdale, NJ: Lawrence Erlbaum.

Courts, B., & Tucker, J. (2012). Using Technology to Create a Dynamic Classroom Experience. *Journal of Teaching and Learning (TLC) 9 (2)* , 121-128.

Geer, R., & Sweeney, T. (2012). Student Voices About Learning With Technology. *Jorunal of Social Sciences 8 (2)*, 294-303.

(2009). *Gen Y's are not yet Taking Flight on Twitter. Welcome to the Participatory Marketing Network.*

Harel, I., & Papert, S. (1991). *Constructionism, 41-48* . Norwood, NJ: Ablex.

Hudson, H. (2011). The Digital Divide. *Instructor, 121 (2)*, 46-50.

Kulik, J. (1994). *Technology Assessment in Education and Training* . Hillsdale, NJ: Lawrence Erlbaum.

Ritchel, M. (21 November 2010). Growing up Digital, Wired for Distraction. *The New York Times* .

Scardamalia, M., & Bereiter, C. (1996). *CSCL: Theory and Practice of an Emerging Paradigm.* Mahwah NJ: Erlbaum.

Sikorsk, J. (2007). *Milestones. The Negative Impact of Baby DVDs.* Los Angeles: Family Magazine Group.

Sivin-Kachala, J. (1998). *Report on the Effectiveness of Technology is Schools, 1990-1997.* Software Publisher's Association.

US Department of Education. *Effects of Technology on Classroom.*

Wenglisky, H. (1998). Does it Compute? The Relationship Between Educational Technology and Student Achievement in Mathematics. *Educational Testing Service Policy Information Center* .

Baldanf, K. J., & Stair, R. M. (2008). *Succeeding with Technology: Computer System Concepts for Real Life.* Cencage Learning.

Bauchspies, W. K., Croissant, J., & Restivo, S. (2005). *Science Technology and Society: A Social Approach.* John Wiley & Sons.

Bergen, D., Reid, R., & Torelli, L. (2007). *Educating and Caring for Very Young Children: The Infant Toddler Curriculum.* Teachers College Press.

Chapelle, C. A. (2003). *English Language Learning and technology: Lectures on Applied Linguistics in the Age of Information and Communication Technology.* John Benjamins Publishing.

Goyder, J. (2005). *Technology and Society: A Canadian Perspective.* University of Toronto.

Green, L. (2002). *Communication, Technology and Society.* SAGE.

Hjorth, L. S. (2003). *Technology and Society: A Bridge to the 21st Century.* Prentice Hall.

Komblum, W., & Smith, C. D. (2007). *Sociology in a Changing .* Cencage Learning.

Nevers, N. D. (1972). *Technology and Society.* Wesley Publications Company.

Pattavina, A. (2004). *Information Technology and the Criminal Justice System.* SAGE.

Universitat zu Koln. (1983). *Asssessing the Impacts of Information Technology.*